50 Special Biscuit Recipes

(50 Special Biscuit Recipes - Volume 1)

Carol Moran

Content

CHAPTER 1: EASY BISCUIT RECIPES 4

1. Alfajores 4
2. Angry Biscuits 4
3. Banoffee S'mores 5
4. Basic Cookies 6
5. Cherry Shortbread Hearts 6
6. Chocolate Bat Biscuits 7
7. Christmas Biscuits 7
8. Coconut Nice 8
9. Crisp Orange Shortbread 9
10. Custard Kisses 9
11. Double Chocolate Shortbreads 10
12. Easiest Ever Biscuits 10
13. Espresso, Hazelnut & Chocolate Shortbread 11
14. Fancy Iced Biscuits 12
15. Ginger Fairings 13
16. Gingerbread Man 13
17. Grandmaster Glitch Chocolate Moustache Biscuits 14
18. Lebkuchen 15
19. Lemon Kisses 15
20. Orange & Ginger Stained Glass Biscuits .. 16
21. Orange, Oat & Sultana Cookies 16
22. Rye & Pumpkin Seed Crackers 17
23. Sea Salt Water Biscuits 17
24. Unicorn Biscuits 18
25. Vegan Gingerbread People 19

CHAPTER 2: AWESOME BISCUIT RECIPES 19

26. Almond & Lemon Curd Buttons 19
27. Basic Biscuit Dough 20
28. Black Tahini Chocolate Cookies 20
29. Bumper Oat Cookies 21
30. Chewy Chocolate Chip Cookies 22
31. Chocolate & Hazelnut Thumbprint Cookies 22
32. Chocolate Chunk Pecan Cookies 23
33. Chocolate Fudge Sprinkle Crinkle Biscuits 23
34. Chocolate Peanut Butter Shortbread Sandwiches 24
35. Coconut & Chocolate Macaroons 25
36. Custard & White Chocolate Biscuits 25
37. Easy Chocolate Biscuits 26
38. Festive Jammie Dodgers 26
39. Freezer Biscuits 27
40. Ginger Cookie Sandwiches With Lemon Mascarpone 28
41. Gooey Chocolate Cherry Cookies 29
42. Lemon Sherbet Jammy Dodgers 29
43. Oat Biscuits 30
44. Oaty Hazelnut Cookies 30
45. Pistachio & Cranberry Cookies 31
46. Shortbread Recipe 31
47. Sugar Dusted Vanilla Shortbread 32
48. Sugared Flower Shortbreads 32
49. Vegan Shortbread 34
50. Viennese Whirls 34

INDEX 36

CONCLUSION 38

Chapter 1: Easy Biscuit Recipes

***

1. Alfajores

Serving: makes 30 | Prep: 45mins | Cook: 20mins | Ready in:

Ingredients

- 200g plain flour
- 300g corn flour
- 2 tsp baking powder
- 250g unsalted butter, softened at room temperature
- 150g caster sugar
- zest of 1 lemon
- 3 large egg yolks
- 1 tbsp cognac
- 1 tsp vanilla extract
- 450g jar dulce de leche
- 50g desiccated coconut

Direction

- Combine the flour, corn flour and baking powder together in a bowl with a pinch of salt. Using a food mixer or an electric whisk in another bowl beat the butter together with the sugar and lemon zest until very pale. Add the egg yolks followed by the Cognac and vanilla extract. Beat in the dry ingredients until you have smooth dough. Wrap the dough in clingfilm and chill for a minimum of 1 hour. You can make the biscuit dough the day before and leave in the fridge.
- Line two large baking trays with baking parchment. Roll out the dough on a lightly floured surface to the thickness of a pound coin then cut out 60 biscuits with a 5cm round or fluted cutter. Put the biscuits back in the fridge for 20 mins to firm up.
- Heat the oven to 180C/160C fan/gas 4. Bake the biscuits for 8 mins until just set. You want the biscuits to stay pale with a crumbly texture. Leave to cool completely before sandwiching two biscuits together with a spoonful of dulce de leche. Once all the biscuits are sandwiched together roll in desiccated coconut.

Nutrition Information

- Calories: 157 calories
- Total Carbohydrate: 21 grams carbohydrates
- Sugar: 9 grams sugar
- Total Fat: 7 grams fat
- Fiber: 0.4 grams fiber
- Sodium: 0.1 milligram of sodium
- Saturated Fat: 5 grams saturated fat
- Protein: 2 grams protein

2. Angry Biscuits

Serving: makes around 40 biscuits | Prep: 15mins | Cook: 30mins | Ready in:

Ingredients

- 200g unsalted butter, at room temperature
- 350g plain flour, plus extra for dusting
- 50g cocoa powder
- 200g golden caster sugar
- 1 egg
- ½ tsp vanilla extract
- 100g dark chocolate chips (or chopped dark chocolate)
- To decorate
- 50g dark chocolate
- 50g white chocolate

- 1-2 balls stem ginger, chopped into small pieces
- pinch chilli flakes
- pinch sea salt flakes

Direction

- Rub the butter and flour together in a large bowl until the mixture represents fine breadcrumbs then stir in the cocoa powder. In another bowl beat together the sugar, egg and vanilla until smooth, then pour over the flour and butter. Knead it together with your hands to form a fairly soft dough then knead in the chocolate chips. Wrap in cling film and chill in the fridge for 20-30 mins.
- Heat oven to 160C/140C fan/gas 3 and line 2 baking sheets with baking parchment. Put the rested dough onto a lightly floured surface and roll it out to about the thickness of a £1 coin. Use a knife, cookie cutter or pizza cutter to chop into shards, or tear it into strips, whatever you feel like. So the biscuits bake evenly, try to make sure they're roughly the same size, ours were between 5-7cm long and 2-5cm wide. Feel free to re-roll the dough as much as you like so you can use it all up.
- Lay the biscuit pieces onto your prepared trays and bake in the oven for 15-17 mins, you may need to do this in 2 batches. Remove from the oven and leave to cool before removing from the parchment. Allow to cool completely on a wire rack before decorating.
- To decorate put the chocolate in separate microwavable bowls and heat each one in 30 sec bursts in the microwave until melted, alternatively set the bowls over pans of barely simmering water until the chocolate has fully melted. Lay all the baked biscuits out on the baking parchment or sheets of foil sitting close together and using a teaspoon, drizzle, pour or splat the melted chocolate over the surface. Sprinkle with the chopped stem ginger, chilli flakes and sea salt if you like. Leave to set completely before serving. Keeps in an airtight container for 2-3 days.

Nutrition Information

- Calories: 110 calories
- Saturated Fat: 3 grams saturated fat
- Total Fat: 6 grams fat
- Sodium: 0.01 milligram of sodium
- Protein: 1 grams protein
- Fiber: 1 grams fiber
- Total Carbohydrate: 13 grams carbohydrates
- Sugar: 6 grams sugar

3. Banoffee S'mores

Serving: Makes 8 | Prep: 3mins | Cook: 2mins | Ready in:

Ingredients

- 16 milk chocolate oat biscuits (we used Milk Chocolate Hobnobs)
- 8 large marshmallows (vegetarian brand, if required)
- 8 tsp dulce de leche
- 1 banana, cut into 16 slices

Direction

- Preheat the grill to high and line a baking sheet with parchment. Put 8 Hobnobs on the tray with a marshmallow on top and grill until slightly brown and melting.
- Put a tsp of dulce de leche on the remaining 8 Hobnobs and top with 2 banana slices. Sandwich the biscuits together.

Nutrition Information

- Calories: 232 calories
- Total Fat: 9 grams fat
- Sugar: 21 grams sugar
- Sodium: 0.3 milligram of sodium
- Total Carbohydrate: 33 grams carbohydrates
- Saturated Fat: 5 grams saturated fat
- Fiber: 2 grams fiber
- Protein: 3 grams protein

4. Basic Cookies

Serving: Makes 25 | Prep: 20mins | Cook: 12mins | Ready in:

Ingredients

- 225g butter, softened
- 110g caster sugar
- 275g plain flour
- 1 tsp cinnamon or other spices (optional)
- 75g white or milk chocolate chips (optional)

Direction

- Heat the oven to 190C/170C fan/gas 5. Cream the butter in a large bowl with a wooden spoon or in a stand mixer until it is soft. Add the sugar and keep beating until the mixture is light and fluffy. Sift in the flour and add the optional ingredients, if you're using them. Bring the mixture together with your hands in a figure-of-eight motion until it forms a dough. You can freeze the dough at this point.
- Roll the dough into walnut-sized balls and place them slightly apart from each other on a baking sheet (you don't need to butter or line it). Flatten the balls a little with the palm of your hand and bake them in the oven for around 10-12 mins until they are golden brown and slightly firm on top. Leave the cookies on a cooling rack for around 15 mins before serving.

Nutrition Information

- Calories: 125 calories
- Protein: 1 grams protein
- Total Fat: 8 grams fat
- Sodium: 0.2 milligram of sodium
- Fiber: 0.4 grams fiber
- Saturated Fat: 5 grams saturated fat
- Sugar: 4 grams sugar
- Total Carbohydrate: 13 grams carbohydrates

5. Cherry Shortbread Hearts

Serving: Makes 14-16, depending on cutter | Prep: 15mins | Cook: 15mins | Ready in:

Ingredients

- 100g icing sugar, plus extra for dusting
- 200g plain flour, plus extra for dusting
- 50g cornflour
- 50g ground almonds
- 250g pack cold butter, cut into cubes
- 50g glacé cherries, finely chopped
- ½ tsp almond extract
- 8 tbsp cherry jam, sieved

Direction

- Heat oven to 180C/160C fan/gas 4. Sift the icing sugar, flour and cornflour together into a bowl. Stir in the ground almonds and butter, then rub in the butter until smooth. Stir in the chopped glacé cherries and almond extract, and bring together to form a dough.
- Roll out on a lightly floured surface, then stamp out biscuits using a heartshaped cutter. Keep re-rolling the trimmings until all the dough is used. Carefully transfer the biscuits to baking trays lined with parchment and bake for just 8-10 mins until just pale golden.
- Using an upturned bottle top or similar, press gently into the centre of each biscuit to make a round indent. Spoon in a little jam and return to the oven for 2 mins. Remove and cool on a wire rack, before dusting with icing sugar to serve.

Nutrition Information

- Calories: 242 calories
- Sodium: 0.21 milligram of sodium
- Fiber: 1 grams fiber
- Saturated Fat: 8 grams saturated fat
- Protein: 2 grams protein
- Total Carbohydrate: 27 grams carbohydrates

- Total Fat: 15 grams fat
- Sugar: 14 grams sugar

6. Chocolate Bat Biscuits

Serving: makes 25-30 biscuits, depending on cutter size | Prep: 10mins | Cook: 10mins | Ready in:

Ingredients

- 125g butter, softened
- 85g icing sugar
- 1large egg yolk
- 1 tsp vanilla extract
- 1 tsp milk
- 175g plain flour, plus extra for rolling
- 1 tsp fine espresso-style powder coffee (I used Azeera)
- 50g cocoa powder
- ¼ tsp salt
- To decorate
- 100g bar dark or milk chocolate
- chocolate hundreds and thousands
- coloured writing icing (or make your own with 100g icing sugar, 3-4 tsp water and some colouring)

Direction

- Heat oven to 180C/160C fan/gas 4 and line two baking sheets with baking parchment. Beat the butter and sugar together until creamy and pale, then beat in the yolk, the vanilla and milk. Sift the flour, coffee, cocoa and salt into the bowl, then mix together to make a soft dough. Shape the dough into a disc, wrap and chill for 15 mins.
- Dust the dough all over with a little flour, then roll it between two large sheets of baking parchment, to the thickness of a £1 coin. Remove the top layer of the paper, stamp shapes with an 8cm bat (or other) cutter, and carefully lift to the lined sheets using a palette knife. Re-roll the trimmings. Cut a 1.5cm x 5mm notch at the base of each bat's body. This is about right to sit the bats on thick tumblers; if your glasses are finer-edged, make the notches thinner so that the bats stay put. Bake for 10 mins or until the biscuits feel sandy and smell rich and chocolatey. Cool on the sheets for 5 mins, then lift the cookies onto a wire rack and cool completely.
- To decorate, melt the chocolate over a pan of simmering water or in the microwave. One biscuit at a time, brush chocolate over the bat ears and wings with a small paintbrush, then cover with chocolate sprinkles. Tap off the excess. Pipe faces and fangs onto your bats, then leave to dry. Keep in an airtight container for up to a week.

Nutrition Information

- Calories: 72 calories
- Sodium: 0.1 milligram of sodium
- Total Carbohydrate: 7 grams carbohydrates
- Fiber: 0.5 grams fiber
- Protein: 1 grams protein
- Total Fat: 4 grams fat
- Saturated Fat: 2 grams saturated fat
- Sugar: 3 grams sugar

7. Christmas Biscuits

Serving: Makes 30-40 depending on size | Prep: 40mins | Cook: 15mins | Ready in:

Ingredients

- 175g dark muscovado sugar
- 85g golden syrup
- 100g butter
- 3 tsp ground ginger
- 1 tsp ground cinnamon
- 350g plain flour, plus extra for dusting
- 1 tsp bicarbonate of soda
- 1 egg, lightly beaten
- To finish
- 100g white chocolate

- edible silver balls

Direction

- Heat the sugar, golden syrup and butter until melted. Mix the spices and flour in a large bowl. Dissolve the bicarbonate of soda in 1 tsp cold water. Make a well in the centre of the dry ingredients, add the melted sugar mix, egg and bicarbonate of soda. Mix well. At this stage the mix will be soft but will firm up on cooling.
- Cover the surface of the biscuit mix with wrapping and leave to cool, then put in the fridge for at least 1 hr to become firm enough to roll out.
- Heat oven to 190C/170C fan/gas 5. Turn the dough out onto a lightly floured surface and knead briefly. (At this stage the dough can be put into a food bag and kept in the fridge for up to a week.) Cut the dough in half. Thinly roll out one half on a lightly floured surface. Cut into shapes with cutters, such as gifts, trees and hearts, then transfer to baking sheets, leaving a little room for them to spread. If you plan to hang the biscuits up, make a small hole in the top of each one using a skewer. Repeat with remaining dough.
- Bake for 12-15 mins until they darken slightly. If the holes you have made have closed up, remake them while the biscuits are warm and soft using a skewer. Cool for a few mins on the baking sheets, then transfer to a wire rack to cool and harden up completely.
- Break up the chocolate and melt in the microwave on Medium for 1-2 mins, or in a small heatproof bowl over simmering water. Drizzle the chocolate over the biscuits, or pipe on shapes or names, then stick a few silver balls into the chocolate. If hung up on the tree, the biscuits will be edible for about a week, but will last a lot longer as decorations.

Nutrition Information

- Calories: 119 calories
- Saturated Fat: 2 grams saturated fat
- Total Carbohydrate: 20 grams carbohydrates
- Sugar: 11 grams sugar
- Protein: 2 grams protein
- Sodium: 0.18 milligram of sodium
- Total Fat: 4 grams fat

8. Coconut Nice

Serving: Makes around 30 | Prep: 30mins | Cook: 40mins | Ready in:

Ingredients

- 1 tbsp linseeds
- 400g plain flour, plus extra for dusting
- 200g coconut oil
- 50g desiccated coconut
- 280g golden caster sugar
- 4 tbsp coconut cream
- 200-225g icing sugar
- 50g desiccated coconut

Direction

- Heat oven to 180C/160C fan/gas 4. Put the linseeds in a small bowl and add 3 tbsp water. Leave to soak for 5-10 mins. Meanwhile, rub the flour and coconut oil together in a large mixing bowl until the coconut oil is well distributed and the mixture looks like fresh breadcrumbs. Stir in the desiccated coconut and set aside.
- Tip the linseeds, together with their soaking water, into the bowl of a mini food processor and blitz until frothy. Add the sugar and blitz again until well mixed. Pour the linseed and sugar mixture into the flour and coconut oil and knead together to form a ball of dough. If the dough feels like it's too dry and may crack when rolling out, add a little water, 1 tsp at a time.
- Transfer the dough to a floured surface and roll it out to about the thickness of a £1 coin. Cut into 7cm x 4cm rectangles and place on a large baking sheet lined with baking

parchment – make sure you leave 2-3cm between each biscuit. Bake in batches for 10-12 mins or until just starting to turn golden at the edges. Transfer to a wire rack using a palette knife or fish slice and leave to cool completely before decorating.

- To decorate, mix together the coconut cream and enough icing sugar to make a thick paste. Transfer to a piping bag and pipe a thin line all around the outside edge of a biscuit, then dip the icing into the desiccated coconut. Repeat with all of the biscuits. Pipe the word 'NICE' onto the middle of each biscuit, then leave to set.

Nutrition Information

- Calories: 174 calories
- Total Fat: 9 grams fat
- Saturated Fat: 8 grams saturated fat
- Total Carbohydrate: 20 grams carbohydrates
- Sugar: 10 grams sugar
- Fiber: 1 grams fiber
- Protein: 2 grams protein

9. Crisp Orange Shortbread

Serving: Easily doubled | Prep: 10mins | Cook: 15mins | Ready in:

Ingredients

- 100g butter, softened
- 50g golden caster sugar
- grated zest ½ orange
- 175g gluten-free flour (try Doves Farm)
- ½ tsp gluten-free baking powder (we used Supercook)

Direction

- Heat oven to 190C/fan 170C/gas 5. Lightly oil a baking sheet. Beat the butter, then cream it with the sugar and orange zest until light. Stir in the flour and baking powder and mix together to form a dough.
- Divide the mixture into 10 balls, arrange on a baking sheet. Press each ball fl at with the tip of a round-bladed knife. Chill for 15 mins, then bake for 12-15 mins until light golden. Leave on the baking sheet for 2 mins before releasing with a palette knife. Slide onto a rack to cool. Will keep stored in an airtight container for up to a week.

Nutrition Information

- Calories: 154 calories
- Protein: 1 grams protein
- Total Fat: 9 grams fat
- Saturated Fat: 5 grams saturated fat
- Total Carbohydrate: 20 grams carbohydrates
- Sugar: 5 grams sugar
- Fiber: 1 grams fiber
- Sodium: 0.2 milligram of sodium

10. Custard Kisses

Serving: Makes 15-25 | Prep: 30mins | Cook: 10mins | Ready in:

Ingredients

- 175g softened butter
- 50g golden caster sugar
- 50g icing sugar
- 2 egg yolks
- 2 tsp vanilla extract
- 300g plain flour, plus extra for dusting
- For the custard filling
- 100g softened butter
- 140g icing sugar, sifted, plus a little extra
- 2 tbsp custard powder
- few drops yellow food colouring, if you have any

Direction

- Heat oven to 200C/180C fan/gas 6. Mix the butter, sugars, egg yolks and vanilla with a wooden spoon until creamy, then mix in the flour in 2 batches. Roll out thinly on a floured surface, then use a standard 30cm ruler as a template to cut the dough into small, even squares. Do this by starting with the ruler flush with one side and cutting along the length of it. Repeat across the width of the dough, then do the same from the top down. Transfer to baking sheets and bake for 8-10 mins until golden.
- While the biscuits cool, mix the butter, icing sugar, custard powder and food colouring, if you have any. Pipe or spread a little icing onto a biscuit, then sandwich with 1 or 2 more biscuits. Repeat until all the biscuits are used, then dust with a little more icing sugar.

Nutrition Information

- Calories: 220 calories
- Total Carbohydrate: 20 grams carbohydrates
- Sugar: 18 grams sugar
- Protein: 1 grams protein
- Sodium: 0.24 milligram of sodium
- Total Fat: 16 grams fat
- Saturated Fat: 10 grams saturated fat

11. Double Chocolate Shortbreads

Serving: Makes 10 | Prep: | Cook: 12mins | Ready in:

Ingredients

- 175g butter, softened
- 85g golden caster sugar
- 200g plain flour
- 2 tbsp cocoa powder
- 100g chocolate chips, milk or dark

Direction

- Mix the butter and sugar together with a wooden spoon. Stir in the flour and cocoa, followed by the chocolate chips – you'll probably need to mix it together with your hands at this stage. Halve the dough and roll each piece into a log about 5cm thick. Wrap in cling film and chill for 1 hr or for several days. Can be frozen for up to 1 month.
- Heat oven to 180C/160C fan/gas 4. Slice logs into 1cm-thick rounds, transfer to a baking tray lined with baking parchment and bake for 10-12 mins. Cool on the tray.

Nutrition Information

- Calories: 290 calories
- Protein: 3 grams protein
- Saturated Fat: 11 grams saturated fat
- Total Carbohydrate: 31 grams carbohydrates
- Total Fat: 18 grams fat
- Fiber: 1 grams fiber
- Sodium: 0.22 milligram of sodium
- Sugar: 15 grams sugar

12. Easiest Ever Biscuits

Serving: makes 24 | Prep: 10mins | Cook: 20mins | Ready in:

Ingredients

- 200g unsalted butter, softened
- 200g golden caster sugar
- 1 large egg
- ½ tsp vanilla extract
- 400g plain flour, plus extra for dusting

Direction

- Heat the oven to 200C/180C fan/gas 6 and line a baking sheet with baking parchment. Put the butter in a bowl and beat it with electric beaters until soft and creamy. Beat in the sugar, then the egg and vanilla, and finally the flour to make a dough. If the dough feels a bit sticky, add a little bit more flour and knead it in.

- Pull pieces off the dough and roll them out to about the thickness of two £1 coins on a floured surface. The easiest way to do this with small children is to roll the mixture out on a baking mat. Cut out shapes using a 9cm biscuit cutter, or a use the rim of a small glass and peel away the leftover dough around the edges. Press some clean toys gently into the biscuits, making sure you make enough of a mark without going all the way through. Re-roll off-cuts and repeat.
- Transfer the whole mat or the individual biscuits to the baking sheet and bake for 8-10 mins or until the edges are just brown. Leave to cool for 5 mins, then serve. Will keep for three days in a biscuit tin.

Nutrition Information

- Calories: 161 calories
- Saturated Fat: 4 grams saturated fat
- Total Carbohydrate: 21 grams carbohydrates
- Sugar: 8 grams sugar
- Fiber: 1 grams fiber
- Protein: 2 grams protein
- Total Fat: 7 grams fat

13. Espresso, Hazelnut & Chocolate Shortbread

Serving: makes 20 | Prep: 50mins | Cook: 30mins | Ready in:

Ingredients

- 2 tbsp instant espresso powder
- 250g butter, softened at room temperature
- 85g caster sugar
- 225g plain flour, plus extra for dusting
- 75g rice flour
- 75g unblanched hazelnuts, halved
- To decorate
- 150g 70% dark chocolate, broken into chunks
- 75g blanched hazelnuts, toasted and very roughly chopped (leave some pieces quite large)

Direction

- Mix the espresso powder with 1 tsp hot water to form a paste (you'll think it isn't enough water but it is - don't add more otherwise it'll be too watery). Set aside.
- Beat the butter and sugar until soft and blended, then beat in the coffee mixture. Don't overbeat the mixture as you don't want to incorporate too much air. (If the coffee isn't completely incorporated, don't worry - it will be once you add the flours).
- Sift together the flours and add them to the butter in three lots, mixing in with a wooden spoon and, eventually, your hands. Bring together into a ball, then transfer to a lightly floured surface and quickly knead in the hazelnuts. Don't overdo this - you don't want the butter to get too warm. Press the dough into a circle, wrap it in cling film and put in the fridge for about 40 mins.
- Roll out the dough on a lightly floured surface to 0.75cm thick. Cut out circles about 6cm across with a biscuit cutter and put the circles on a non-stick baking sheet (or two baking sheets, depending on their size). Re-roll the dough as you need to, but try not to do this too often. Put the baking sheets in the coldest part of the fridge and leave them for about 45 mins. Heat oven to 160C/140C fan/gas 3.
- Bake the shortbread for 20 mins, or until the top is just firm when you press it with your index finger. Take out of the oven and leave on the baking sheets to cool for a while (it is very fragile when hot), then transfer to a wire rack to cool completely.
- Melt the chocolate in a bowl set over a pan of simmering water, then remove the bowl and leave to cool a little and rm up somewhat. Dip each piece of shortbread halfway in the melted chocolate, then put on a sheet of baking parchment. Sprinkle the toasted hazelnuts on

the chocolate half and leave to set completely. Will keep for 4 days in an airtight tin.

Nutrition Information

- Calories: 259 calories
- Total Carbohydrate: 19 grams carbohydrates
- Fiber: 2 grams fiber
- Total Fat: 18 grams fat
- Saturated Fat: 9 grams saturated fat
- Sodium: 0.2 milligram of sodium
- Sugar: 6 grams sugar
- Protein: 3 grams protein

14. Fancy Iced Biscuits

Serving: Makes 20 | Prep: 1hours | Cook: 17mins | Ready in:

Ingredients

- For lime & vanilla biscuits
- 300g plain flour
- ¼ tsp salt
- 150g golden caster sugar
- zest 3 limes
- 150g cold unsalted butter, diced
- 1 large egg
- 1 tsp vanilla bean paste
- To decorate
- 400g royal icing sugar
- juice 1-2 lemons (about 75ml), or 2-4 limes
- gel food colouring - we used orange, pink and yellow

Direction

- Line a couple of trays with baking parchment and heat oven to 180C/160C fan/gas 4. Mix together the flour, salt, caster sugar and lime zest (keep the zested limes for the icing). Add the butter and rub together until the mixture resembles fine breadcrumbs.
- Beat the egg and vanilla bean paste together with a fork, then mix into the other ingredients. Knead until even. Chill until firm, then roll on a lightly floured surface until about 4-5mm thick. Stamp out 8cm rounds, transfer to baking trays, then chill again for 15 mins before baking for 15-17 mins until golden. Remove from the oven, transfer to a wire rack and leave to cool before decorating.
- For the icing, put the royal icing sugar into a bowl, add about 65ml lemon or lime juice and use a metal spoon or electric mixer to beat until it is fairly thick and glossy. If the icing is too thick though, it will be hard to pipe. Take a quarter of the icing, put into a piping bag fitted with a No 2 (very small round) piping nozzle and set aside. To see step-by-step images, please see the tips, below left, for a link to our guide page.
- For the flood icing, add another 10ml lemon or lime juice to the remaining icing, a few drops at a time until it is pourable. You can now divide this icing into as many bowls as you like and colour by mixing in a little gel food colouring.
- Place the coloured icing into three piping bags, ready for decorating.
- To decorate the biscuits, use the thicker icing to draw your outline or design onto the biscuits. Let the icing set for a few minutes.
- Pipe enough runnier icing to cover the entire biscuit - don't worry about it being neat at this point. Use a toothpick to spread the icing evenly inside the hard icing 'wall'. If the surface of the icing isn't flat, gently shake the biscuit back and forth until you have a smooth covering.
- To add a simple dot decoration, while the icing is still wet, use the runnier icing again to pipe dots again - this will sink on, leaving you with a smooth effect. Pop the biscuits onto a baking tray and place into an oven at its lowest setting for about 30 mins to allow the icing to set hard.

Nutrition Information

- Calories: 210 calories
- Fiber: 1 grams fiber
- Total Fat: 7 grams fat
- Total Carbohydrate: 36 grams carbohydrates
- Saturated Fat: 4 grams saturated fat
- Protein: 2 grams protein
- Sugar: 25 grams sugar
- Sodium: 0.1 milligram of sodium

15. Ginger Fairings

Serving: Makes 16 | Prep: 10mins | Cook: 10mins | Ready in:

Ingredients

- 100g butter, diced, plus extra for the baking sheet
- 225g plain flour
- 2 tsp baking powder
- 2 tsp bicarbonate of soda
- 1 tbsp ground ginger
- 2 tsp mixed spice
- 100g caster sugar
- 4 tbsp golden syrup

Direction

- Heat oven to 200C/180C fan/gas 6. Lightly butter 2 large baking sheets. Put the flour, ¼ tsp salt, baking powder, bicarb and spices in a food processor. Add the diced butter and whizz until the mixture resembles breadcrumbs. Tip into a bowl and stir in the sugar.
- Gently warm the golden syrup in a pan, add to the mixture and stir to form a dough. Roll the dough into 16 walnut-sized balls, then arrange, at least 2cm apart, on the baking sheets. Bake for 8-10 mins until golden. Cool on the trays before transferring to a wire rack.

Nutrition Information

- Calories: 136 calories
- Total Carbohydrate: 21 grams carbohydrates
- Total Fat: 5 grams fat
- Sodium: 0.6 milligram of sodium
- Fiber: 1 grams fiber
- Saturated Fat: 3 grams saturated fat
- Sugar: 10 grams sugar
- Protein: 2 grams protein

16. Gingerbread Man

Serving: Makes 12 big gingerbread men | Prep: 45mins | Cook: 15mins | Ready in:

Ingredients

- 140g unsalted butter
- 100g dark muscovado sugar
- 3 tbsp golden syrup
- 350g plain flour
- 1 tsp bicarbonate of soda
- 2 tsp ground ginger
- 1 tsp ground cinnamon
- pinch of cayenne pepper (optional)
- 2 balls stem ginger from a jar, chopped
- To decorate
- 50g icing sugar
- a few glacé cherries (we used undyed)
- 2 balls stem ginger

Direction

- Heat oven to 200C/180C fan/gas 6. Line 2 baking sheets with baking parchment. Melt butter, sugar and syrup in a pan. Mix flour, soda, spices and a pinch of salt in a bowl. Stir in the butter mix and chopped ginger to make a stiff-ish dough.
- Wait until cool enough to handle, then roll out dough to about 5mm thick. Stamp out gingerbread men, re-rolling and pressing the trimmings back together and rolling again. Lift onto baking sheets. Bake for 12 mins until golden. Cool 10 mins on the sheets, then lift onto cooling racks.

- To decorate, mix icing sugar with a few drops of water until thick and smooth. Halve then slice cherries thinly to make smiles, and cut ginger into small squares. Spoon icing into a food bag, snip off the tiniest bit from one corner, then squeeze eyes and buttons, and a tiny smile onto 1 man at a time. Stick on a cherry smile and ginger buttons. Repeat; leave to set. Will keep up to 1 week in an airtight tin.

Nutrition Information

- Calories: 264 calories
- Protein: 3 grams protein
- Fiber: 1 grams fiber
- Sodium: 0.33 milligram of sodium
- Saturated Fat: 6 grams saturated fat
- Total Carbohydrate: 43 grams carbohydrates
- Sugar: 20 grams sugar
- Total Fat: 10 grams fat

17. Grandmaster Glitch Chocolate Moustache Biscuits

Serving: makes 25 biscuits | Prep: 1hours | Cook: 20mins | Ready in:

Ingredients

- 125g salted butter, softened
- 125g caster sugar
- 1 medium egg, lightly beaten
- 1 tsp vanilla extract
- 200g plain flour
- 50g cocoa powder
- You will also need
- moustache biscuit cutter or template cut from a piece of card
- wooden coffee stirrer sticks
- 100g melted milk chocolate or dark chocolate
- chocolate sprinkles

Direction

- Heat the oven to 180C/160C fan/gas 4 and line two baking sheets with parchment. Cream together the butter and sugar, then gradually beat in the egg and vanilla extract. Sift and stir in the flour and cocoa powder and mix to a fairly soft dough. Turn onto a lightly floured surface and knead gently. Cover or wrap the dough in cling film and chill for at least 30-60 minutes.
- When ready, roll the dough out on a lightly floured surface to around the thickness of 0.5cm. Cut out the moustaches using either the template or a moustache biscuit cutter.
- Carefully transfer the biscuits to the lined baking sheets using a spatula and carefully poke a coffee stirrer stick into the bottom of each biscuit. Repeat with the remaining dough, re-rolling the trimmings to make more biscuits. Note: you may need to use more trays or bake the biscuits in batches due to the coffee stirrer sticks taking up room on the baking sheets.
- Bake the biscuits for approximately 10-12 minutes. Leave the biscuits to firm up on their trays before transferring to a wire rack to cool.
- Apply the melted chocolate to the front of each biscuit using a paintbrush and sprinkle with chocolate strands. Leave to set before enjoying with a selfie!

Nutrition Information

- Calories: 188 calories
- Protein: 2 grams protein
- Saturated Fat: 4 grams saturated fat
- Sugar: 7 grams sugar
- Total Carbohydrate: 14 grams carbohydrates
- Fiber: 1 grams fiber
- Sodium: 0.1 milligram of sodium
- Total Fat: 6 grams fat

18. Lebkuchen

Serving: Makes 30 | Prep: 15mins | Cook: 15mins | Ready in:

Ingredients

- 250g plain flour
- 85g ground almond
- 2 tsp ground ginger
- 1 tsp ground cinnamon
- ½ tsp bicarbonate of soda
- 200ml clear honey
- 1 lemon, finely grated zest
- 85g butter
- pinch each ground cloves, grated nutmeg and black pepper
- 1 tsp baking powder
- For the icing
- 100g icing sugar
- 1 egg white, beaten

Direction

- Tip the dry ingredients into a large bowl. Heat the honey and butter in a pan over a low heat until the butter melts, then pour into the flour mixture along with the lemon zest. Mix well until the dough is combined and fairly solid. Cover and leave to cool.
- Heat oven to 180C/fan160C/gas 4. Using your hands, roll dough into about 30 balls, each 3cm wide, then flatten each one slightly into a disk. Divide the biscuits between two baking trays lined with baking parchment, leaving room for them to expand. Bake for 15 mins, then cool on a wire rack.
- To ice the biscuits, mix together the icing sugar, egg white and 1-2 tbsp water to form a smooth, runny icing. Dip the top of each biscuit in the icing and spread with the back of a knife. Leave to dry out in a warm room.

Nutrition Information

- Calories: 102 calories
- Total Fat: 4 grams fat
- Saturated Fat: 2 grams saturated fat
- Sugar: 9 grams sugar
- Fiber: 0.5 grams fiber
- Total Carbohydrate: 16 grams carbohydrates
- Sodium: 0.16 milligram of sodium
- Protein: 2 grams protein

19. Lemon Kisses

Serving: Makes 20 | Prep: 30mins | Cook: 12mins | Ready in:

Ingredients

- 200g soft butter
- 140g caster sugar
- 1 egg yolk
- 1 tsp vanilla extract
- zest 2 lemons, juice 1
- 280g plain flour, plus a little extra for rolling
- ½ jar good lemon curd(we used Tiptree)
- 140g icing sugar, sifted

Direction

- Stir together the butter, sugar, egg yolk, vanilla and zest from 1 lemon using a wooden spoon. Stir in the flour – you might need to get your hands in at the end. Tip onto a floured surface, bring together into a smooth dough, then roll out, half at a time, and stamp out 5-6cm rounds. Keep re-rolling trimmings, you should get about 40 biscuits. Arrange on trays lined with baking parchment, cover with cling film and chill for 30 mins.
- Heat oven to 200C/180C fan/gas 6. Bake the biscuits for 8-12 mins until pale golden, then cool. Once cool, spread half the biscuits with a little lemon curd and top with a second biscuit. Arrange the biscuits on wire racks over trays. Mix enough lemon juice into the icing sugar to give a runny consistency, then drizzle over the biscuits. Scatter over a bit more lemon zest and leave to set.

Nutrition Information

- Calories: 202 calories
- Total Carbohydrate: 31 grams carbohydrates
- Total Fat: 8 grams fat
- Saturated Fat: 5 grams saturated fat
- Fiber: 1 grams fiber
- Protein: 1 grams protein
- Sodium: 0.14 milligram of sodium
- Sugar: 18 grams sugar

20. Orange & Ginger Stained Glass Biscuits

Serving: Makes 14 | Prep: 15mins | Cook: 20mins | Ready in:

Ingredients

- sunflower oil, for greasing
- 175g plain flour, plus extra
- 1 tsp ground ginger
- zest 1 orange
- 100g butter, cold, cut into chunks
- 50g golden caster sugar
- 1 tbsp milk
- 12 fruit-flavoured boiled sweets
- icing sugar, to dust
- about 120cm thin ribbon, to decorate

Direction

- Heat oven to 180C/fan 160C/gas 4. Grease 2 large non-stick baking sheets with oil. Whizz the flour, ginger, zest and butter with 1/2 tsp salt to fine crumbs in a food processor. Pulse in the sugar and milk, then turn out and knead briefly on a floured surface until smooth. Wrap then chill for about 30 mins.
- Flour the work surface again, then roll out the dough to the thickness of a £1 coin. Use 7cm cutters to cut out shapes, then use 4cm cutters to cut out the middles. Re-roll leftover pieces. Make a hole in the top of each biscuit, then carefully lift onto the baking sheets.
- Crush the sweets in their wrappers with a rolling pin, then put the pieces into the middles of the biscuits - the sweets should be level with the top of the dough. Bake for 15-20 mins or until the biscuits are golden brown and the middles have melted.
- Leave to harden, then transfer to a rack to cool. Thread with ribbon, then dust with icing sugar. Will keep for a month, but best eaten within 3 days.

Nutrition Information

- Calories: 160 calories
- Fiber: 1 grams fiber
- Protein: 2 grams protein
- Sodium: 0.14 milligram of sodium
- Total Fat: 8 grams fat
- Total Carbohydrate: 23 grams carbohydrates
- Sugar: 10 grams sugar
- Saturated Fat: 5 grams saturated fat

21. Orange, Oat & Sultana Cookies

Serving: Makes 16 | Prep: 30mins | Cook: 20mins | Ready in:

Ingredients

- 100g butter at room temperature
- 1 egg
- 50g mashed ripe banana
- 1 tsp vanilla extract
- 100g light soft brown sugar
- ½ tsp grated orange zest
- 100g wholemeal flour
- ¼ tsp salt
- 1 tsp baking powder
- 100g rolled oats
- 25g desiccated coconut
- 50g chopped walnut
- 75g sultana or dark chocolate chips

Direction

- Heat oven to 180C/160C fan/gas 4. Cream the butter and sugar together until well blended and smooth. Gradually beat in the banana, vanilla extract and egg. Add the zest. Mix well with a wooden spoon until thoroughly blended.
- In a large bowl, mix the flour, salt, baking powder, oats, coconut, walnuts and sultanas or chocolate chips. Stir the dry ingredients into the wet and mix thoroughly until a thick dough is formed. Line a baking sheet with parchment. Drop heaped tbsps onto the sheet, leaving a 5cm (2in) space around each one, and press down lightly. Bake for 15-20 mins until lightly browned. Cool.

Nutrition Information

- Calories: 167 calories
- Total Carbohydrate: 19 grams carbohydrates
- Protein: 3 grams protein
- Total Fat: 9 grams fat
- Sugar: 11 grams sugar
- Fiber: 2 grams fiber
- Sodium: 0.18 milligram of sodium
- Saturated Fat: 5 grams saturated fat

22. Rye & Pumpkin Seed Crackers

Serving: Makes 24 | Prep: 20mins | Cook: 1hours30mins | Ready in:

Ingredients

- 200g ryeflour
- 200g wholemeal flour
- 100g pumpkin seed
- ½ tsp baking powder
- 1 tsp salt
- 1 tsp golden caster sugar
- 1 large egg

Direction

- Heat oven to 140C/120C fan/gas 1 and line 2 baking trays with baking parchment. Mix the dry ingredients in a large bowl. Beat the egg with 250ml water in a jug, then pour into the dry mixture. Combine with a wooden spoon, then transfer to a lightly floured work surface and knead until you have a smooth, firm dough.
- Roll the dough out as thinly as possible and cut into squares, about 7cm. Transfer the squares to your baking trays. Bake for 45 mins, then remove the trays from the oven. Flip each cracker over on the tray and return to the oven, swapping over the shelves, for a further 45 mins. Once cooked, remove from the oven and transfer to a wire rack to cool. Store in a sealed container for up to 2 weeks.

Nutrition Information

- Calories: 81 calories
- Total Fat: 3 grams fat
- Total Carbohydrate: 12 grams carbohydrates
- Fiber: 3 grams fiber
- Protein: 3 grams protein
- Sodium: 0.2 milligram of sodium

23. Sea Salt Water Biscuits

Serving: 18 biscuits | Prep: 15mins | Cook: 15mins | Ready in:

Ingredients

- 200g plain flour
- ½ tsp baking powder
- 50g butter, cold, cut into cubes
- flaky sea salt

Direction

- Heat oven to 180C/fan 160C/gas 4. Line two baking sheets with parchment. Place the flour, baking powder, butter and ½ tsp of the flaky salt in a food processor, then whizz for a

minute until the butter is completely mixed with the flour. Add 4 tbsp water and pulse until the dough comes together. If it still feels dry, add 1 tsp more water and process until you have a soft but not sticky dough.
- Roll out the dough on a lightly floured surface into a rectangle approximately 50 x 25cm and as thin as possible. Brush a little water over the surface of the dough, scatter 1 tsp salt flakes over and press in lightly. Prick the dough all over with a fork, then cut into 18 squares. Place on the prepared trays - don't worry if they stretch a bit. Bake for 10-15 mins until the biscuits feel dry and sandy but are still pale - they may still feel soft but will harden up when cooling. Transfer to a wire rack and leave until completely cool. Will keep in an airtight container for up to 2 weeks.

Nutrition Information

- Calories: 59 calories
- Total Fat: 2 grams fat
- Total Carbohydrate: 9 grams carbohydrates
- Protein: 1 grams protein
- Sodium: 0.36 milligram of sodium

24. Unicorn Biscuits

Serving: around 20 | Prep: 15mins | Cook: 30mins | Ready in:

Ingredients

- 250g plain flour
- 150g butter
- 100g caster sugar
- 1 egg
- ½ tsp vanilla extract
- pink food colouring
- 50g icing sugar
- 1 lemon, juice only
- your choice of coloured sprinkles (we used hundreds and thousands, pink and yellow sugar and some white chocolate stars)

Direction

- Rub the flour and butter together with your fingertips until it looks and feels like fresh breadcrumbs then add a pinch of salt. In another bowl, mix together the sugar, egg and vanilla extract then pour it over the butter and flour mixture. Gently knead it together then separate the dough into 2 equal blocks. Knead some pink food colouring into one of them and keep the other plain. Wrap both types of dough in sheets of cling film and chill in the fridge for 20-30 mins.
- Roll the plain dough out onto a lightly floured surface until it's about 25cm long and 20cm wide. Do the same with the pink dough and lay one on top of the other. Lightly roll over the surface once or twice with your rolling pin just to press them together. Trim off all the edges so they're straight then carefully roll them up from one of the short edges to make a tight spiral. Wrap tightly in cling film and chill for 1hr or overnight.
- Heat oven to 180C/160C fan/gas 4 and line 2 trays with baking parchment. Unwrap the dough, trim the end and cut the rest into 20 slices and lay them cut side down on your prepared baking tray. Bake for 15-17 mins or until ever so slightly golden at the very edges. Allow them to cool on the tray before transferring them to a wire rack to cool completely.
- Mix the icing sugar with enough lemon juice to make it the consistency of smooth peanut butter and pour the sprinkles into a shallow bowl or plate. Dip the outside edges of the biscuits into the icing (or spread it onto the edges using the back of a teaspoon) and then into the sprinkles, turning to coat. Leave to set before serving.

Nutrition Information

- Calories: 136 calories
- Total Carbohydrate: 17 grams carbohydrates
- Sugar: 8 grams sugar
- Total Fat: 7 grams fat
- Saturated Fat: 4 grams saturated fat
- Sodium: 0.15 milligram of sodium
- Protein: 2 grams protein
- Fiber: 1 grams fiber

25. Vegan Gingerbread People

Serving: makes around 20 | Prep: 30mins | Cook: 12mins | Ready in:

Ingredients

- 1 tbsp chia seeds
- 400g plain flour, plus extra for dusting
- 200g coconut oil
- 2 tbsp ground ginger
- 1 tsp ground cinnamon
- 200g dark muscovado sugar
- 50g maple syrup
- 100ml aquafaba (water from a can of chickpeas)
- 500g icing sugar
- ½ tsp lemon juice

Direction

- Put the chia seeds in a small bowl and stir in 3 tbsp water. Leave to soak for 5-10 mins until gloopy. Meanwhile put the flour into a large mixing bowl and rub in the coconut oil until it's almost disappeared into the flour. Stir in the spices.
- In another bowl mix together the sugar, maple syrup, chia mixture and 2 tbsp water until smooth then pour over the flour. Stir until well combined then knead together to make a soft dough. Wrap in cling film until ready to use.
- Heat oven to 180C/160C fan/gas 6. Roll out the dough on a lightly floured surface then cut into gingerbread people (or whatever shape you like) and bake for 10-12 mins on baking sheets lined with baking parchment until just starting to darken at the edges. Let them cool for a couple of minutes on the tray then transfer to a wire rack to cool.
- While the gingerbread cools whip the aquafaba in a bowl using electric beaters until really foamy. Add 3/4 of the icing sugar and whisk until smooth and thick, then whisk in the rest of the icing sugar and the lemon juice. Whisk again until the mixture forms stiff peaks. Transfer to a piping bag until ready to use. Snip a little off the end of the piping bag and use to create designs and faces on your gingerbread.

Nutrition Information

- Calories: 315 calories
- Total Fat: 10 grams fat
- Saturated Fat: 9 grams saturated fat
- Fiber: 1 grams fiber
- Sugar: 36 grams sugar
- Protein: 2 grams protein
- Sodium: 0.01 milligram of sodium
- Total Carbohydrate: 52 grams carbohydrates

Chapter 2: Awesome Biscuit Recipes

***

26. Almond & Lemon Curd Buttons

Serving: Makes about 20 | Prep: 15mins | Cook: 15mins | Ready in:

Ingredients

- 250g butter, softened
- 140g golden caster sugar, plus extra

- 1 egg
- 1 tsp vanilla extract
- zest 2 lemons
- 300g plain flour
- 100g ground almond
- a little milk, to seal
- about 3 tbsp lemon curd
- flaked almonds, for the top

Direction

- Heat oven to 190C/fan 170C/gas 5. Beat the butter, sugar, egg, vanilla, zest and a pinch of salt in a large bowl until smooth, then fold in the flour and ground almonds. Shape into 2 rounds, flatten them, then wrap in cling film and chill until firm, about 30 mins.
- Roll out 1 piece of dough on a floured surface to about £1 thickness, then stamp out rounds with a 7cm cutter. Brush all over with milk, then spoon 20p-size blobs of lemon curd into the middle of half of the rounds.
- Carefully lay the remaining rounds on top of the lemon curd, then gently press around the edges with your fingers to seal. Scatter with a little caster sugar and the flaked almonds. Bake for 15 mins until light golden. Repeat with remaining pastry, then squish any offcuts together and re-roll. You can freeze the biscuits before baking, but add up to 5 mins more to the cooking time.

Nutrition Information

- Calories: 225 calories
- Total Fat: 15 grams fat
- Sugar: 10 grams sugar
- Protein: 3 grams protein
- Sodium: 0.21 milligram of sodium
- Saturated Fat: 7 grams saturated fat
- Total Carbohydrate: 22 grams carbohydrates
- Fiber: 1 grams fiber

27. Basic Biscuit Dough

Serving: Makes about 30 cookies | Prep: | Cook: 15mins | Ready in:

Ingredients

- 250g butter, softened
- 140g caster sugar
- 1 egg yolk
- 2 tsp vanilla extract
- 300g plain flour

Direction

- Mix the butter and sugar in a large bowl with a wooden spoon, then add the egg yolk and vanilla extract and briefly beat to combine.
- Sift over the flour and stir until the mixture is well combined – you might need to get your hands in at the end to give everything a really good mix and press the dough together.

Nutrition Information

- Calories: 118 calories
- Protein: 1 grams protein
- Sodium: 0.13 milligram of sodium
- Total Fat: 7 grams fat
- Saturated Fat: 4 grams saturated fat
- Total Carbohydrate: 13 grams carbohydrates
- Sugar: 5 grams sugar

28. Black Tahini Chocolate Cookies

Serving: makes 20 | Prep: 20mins | Cook: 8mins | Ready in:

Ingredients

- 50g salted butter, softened
- 125g light brown muscovado sugar
- 125g golden caster sugar
- 1 egg, beaten
- 200g self-raising flour

- 2 tbsp cocoa powder
- 200g milk chocolate, broken into chunks
- 100g white chocolate, melted, for drizzling
- For the black tahini
- 100g black sesame seeds (available at Waitrose), plus extra for decorating
- 100g flavourless oil
- 30g maple syrup

Direction

- First, make the black tahini. Toast the sesame seeds in a small pan over a gentle heat until you can smell the sesame aroma. Transfer to a mini processor and blitz. Pour in the oil gradually until a paste forms. Add the maple syrup and blitz again. Tip into a small bowl until ready to use.
- Heat oven to 180C/160C fan/gas 4 and line two baking sheets with parchment. In a large bowl, beat the butter and sugars together until pale and fluffy. Add the egg and 80g of black tahini paste, and beat to combine. Tip in the flour, cocoa and milk chocolate chunks, and beat until fully incorporated.
- Using an ice cream scoop, ball the dough into about 20 pieces and place on the baking sheets. Press each ball lightly so it's a little flatter, leaving plenty of room between them, as they will spread.
- Bake for 6-8 mins until still soft in the middle – they will harden as they cool. Leave to cool on the sheets for a few mins before transferring to wire racks to cool completely.
- Once cooled, drizzle white chocolate zigzags all over the cookies and sprinkle some black sesame seeds on top. Will keep in an airtight container for 3 days.

Nutrition Information

- Calories: 254 calories
- Protein: 3 grams protein
- Total Fat: 13 grams fat
- Saturated Fat: 5 grams saturated fat
- Sugar: 21 grams sugar
- Fiber: 1 grams fiber
- Sodium: 0.2 milligram of sodium
- Total Carbohydrate: 29 grams carbohydrates

29. Bumper Oat Cookies

Serving: Makes 18 | Prep: | Cook: | Ready in:

Ingredients

- 175g butter
- 175g demerara sugar
- 100g golden syrup
- 85g plain flour
- ½ tsp bicarbonate of soda
- 250g porridge oats
- 1 tsp ground cinnamon
- 100g each of ready-to-eat dried apricots, chopped and stem ginger, chopped
- 75-80g pack dried sour cherries
- 2 tbsp boiling water
- 1 medium egg, beaten

Direction

- Heat the oven to 180C/fan160C/gas 4. Line several baking sheets with baking parchment or non-stick sheets. Warm the butter, sugar and golden syrup in a large saucepan over a medium heat until the butter has melted. Stir in the flour, bicarbonate of soda, oats, cinnamon, dried fruits and ginger, then the water and finally the egg. Leave to cool until easy to handle.
- With dampened hands, shape the mixture into 18 large balls, then flatten them onto the baking sheets – allowing plenty of space for spreading – and bake for 15-20 mins until golden. (This will give a soft, chewy cookie. For a crisper one, reduce the heat to 160C/fan140C/gas 3 and bake for a further 5-10 mins.)
- Allow the cookies to cool on the trays briefly, then lift onto to a cooling rack. Will keep in an airtight container, separated with baking parchment, for up to 1 week.

Nutrition Information

- Calories: 236 calories
- Saturated Fat: 5 grams saturated fat
- Total Fat: 10 grams fat
- Fiber: 2 grams fiber
- Total Carbohydrate: 37 grams carbohydrates
- Sugar: 13 grams sugar
- Protein: 3 grams protein
- Sodium: 0.3 milligram of sodium

30. Chewy Chocolate Chip Cookies

Serving: Makes 12 | Prep: 10mins | Cook: 10mins | Ready in:

Ingredients

- 150g butter, softened
- 150g soft brown sugar, golden caster sugar, or ideally half of each
- 1 egg
- 1 tsp vanilla extract
- 180-200g plain flour (see tip below)
- ½ tsp baking powder
- 200g chocolate chips or chopped chocolate

Direction

- Mix the butter and sugar together using an electric whisk or hand whisk until very light and fluffy, then beat in the egg and vanilla. Fold in the flour, baking powder, chocolate and ¼ tsp salt as quickly as you can. Don't overwork the dough as this will toughen the cookies.
- For the best flavour, leave the mixture overnight: either cover the bowl and chill, or roll the mixture into balls and chill.
- Heat the oven to 180C/160C fan/gas 4 and line two baking sheets with parchment. Divide the mixture into balls, the craggier the balls, the rougher the cookies will look. If you want to give the dough more texture, tear the balls in half and squidge them lightly back together. Space out evenly on the baking sheets, leaving enough space between each to allow for spreading.
- Bake the fresh cookies for 8-10 mins and the chilled ones for 10-12 mins, or until browned and a little crisp at the edges but still very soft in the middle - they will harden a little as they cool. Leave to cool on the tray for a few minutes before eating warm, or transfer to a wire rack to cool completely. Will keep for three days in an airtight container.

Nutrition Information

- Calories: 299 calories
- Sugar: 18 grams sugar
- Protein: 3 grams protein
- Fiber: 2 grams fiber
- Sodium: 0.4 milligram of sodium
- Total Fat: 17 grams fat
- Total Carbohydrate: 31 grams carbohydrates
- Saturated Fat: 10 grams saturated fat

31. Chocolate & Hazelnut Thumbprint Cookies

Serving: Makes 25 | Prep: 20mins | Cook: 20mins | Ready in:

Ingredients

- 180g hazelnuts, toasted
- 100g plain flour
- 90g buckwheat flour
- 60g golden caster sugar
- 180g unsalted butter
- 100g dark chocolate, roughly chopped
- 1 tsp coconut oil (or use any flavourless oil)

Direction

- Line a baking tray with baking parchment. Tip the hazelnuts into the bowl of a food processor and pulse until finely chopped. Add the flours, sugar and a pinch of flaked sea salt, and process for 20-30 secs until fully combined. Add the butter and pulse until the mixture just starts to come together. Tip the dough out onto a work surface and knead by hand until smooth.
- Roll the dough into 25 small balls, then transfer to the prepared baking tray. Using your thumb or the handle of a wooden spoon, make an indent in the centre of each piece of dough. Put the tray in the fridge and chill for 30 mins before baking. Heat oven to 180C/160C fan/gas 4.
- Bake in the oven for 15-20 mins or until light golden brown. Put the chocolate and oil in a heatproof bowl and set over a pan of simmering water, stirring occasionally, until fully melted. Use a teaspoon to top each cookie with a little melted chocolate. Put aside until the chocolate has set.

Nutrition Information

- Calories: 163 calories
- Fiber: 1 grams fiber
- Protein: 2 grams protein
- Total Fat: 12 grams fat
- Saturated Fat: 5 grams saturated fat
- Total Carbohydrate: 9 grams carbohydrates
- Sugar: 4 grams sugar

32. Chocolate Chunk Pecan Cookies

Serving: Makes 12 | Prep: | Cook: 12mins | Ready in:

Ingredients

- 200g dark chocolate, broken into squares (we like Green & Black's)
- 100g butter, chopped
- 50g light muscovado sugar
- 85g golden caster sugar
- 1 tsp vanilla extract
- 1 egg, beaten
- 100g whole pecan
- 100g plain flour
- 1 tsp bicarbonate of soda

Direction

- Heat oven to 180C/fan 160C/gas 4. Melt 85g chocolate in the microwave on High for 1 min or over a pan of simmering water.
- Beat in the butter, sugars, vanilla and egg until smooth, then stir in three-quarters of both the nuts and remaining chocolate, then the flour and bicarbonate of soda.
- Heap 12 spoonfuls, spaced apart, on 2 baking sheets (don't spread the mixture), then poke in the reserved nuts and chocolate. Bake for 12 mins until firm, then leave to cool on the sheets. Can be stored in a tin for up to 3 days.

Nutrition Information

- Calories: 294 calories
- Total Fat: 20 grams fat
- Sodium: 0.44 milligram of sodium
- Saturated Fat: 8 grams saturated fat
- Total Carbohydrate: 27 grams carbohydrates
- Sugar: 17 grams sugar
- Protein: 4 grams protein
- Fiber: 2 grams fiber

33. Chocolate Fudge Sprinkle Crinkle Biscuits

Serving: Makes 35-40 mini biscuits | Prep: 20mins | Cook: 10mins | Ready in:

Ingredients

- 60g cocoa powder, sieved
- 200g caster sugar

- 60ml vegetable oil
- 2 large eggs
- 180g plain flour
- 1 tsp baking powder
- 1 small tub sprinkles

Direction

- Mix the cocoa, caster sugar and oil together. Whisk in the eggs one at a time, until fully combined.
- Mix the flour, baking powder and a pinch of salt together in a separate bowl, then add to the cocoa mixture and mix until you form a soft dough. If the dough feels very soft, transfer it to the fridge and chill for 1 hr.
- Heat the oven to 190C/170C fan/gas 5 and line a baking tray with baking parchment. Tip the sprinkles into a shallow dish. Form a heaped teaspoon of the dough into a ball, then roll in the sprinkles to coat – you might have to press the sprinkles on, particularly if you've chilled the dough. If they're not sticking well, roll the balls of dough between your hands until the mixture warms up a little. Repeat with the remaining dough, then put, evenly spaced, on the baking tray.
- Bake in the centre of the oven for 10 mins – they will crinkle as they cook. The biscuits will firm up as they cool so don't overcook them. Transfer to a wire rack and leave to cool. Will keep for four days in a biscuit tin.

Nutrition Information

- Calories: 72 calories
- Total Carbohydrate: 11 grams carbohydrates
- Saturated Fat: 1 grams saturated fat
- Sodium: 0.05 milligram of sodium
- Total Fat: 3 grams fat
- Fiber: 1 grams fiber
- Protein: 1 grams protein
- Sugar: 7 grams sugar

34. Chocolate Peanut Butter Shortbread Sandwiches

Serving: Makes about 16 | Prep: 20mins | Cook: 25mins | Ready in:

Ingredients

- For the shortbread
- 150g golden icing sugar
- 225g butter, at room temperature
- 300g plain flour, sifted, plus extra for dusting
- 55g cocoa powder, sifted
- For the peanut buttercream
- 300g golden icing sugar
- 50g butter, at room temperature
- 100g smooth peanut butter
- 2-3 tbsp milk

Direction

- Put everything for the shortbread in a food processor with a pinch of salt and pulse until the mixture comes together to form a dough. If it won't come together, take it out of the processor and bring it together with your hands. Tip onto a lightly floured work surface and shape into a log about 5cm in diameter. Wrap in cling film and chill for 1 hr.
- Heat oven to 140C/120C fan/gas 2. Line two large baking sheets with baking parchment. Cut the log into about 32 rounds 6mm thick and line them up on the sheets. Bake for 22-25 mins. Leave to cool a little, then carefully remove and put on a wire rack to cool completely.
- To make the buttercream, blitz all the ingredients in a food mixer or beat with an electric whisk, adding enough of the milk to make a soft mixture. Sandwich the shortbread together with the buttercream.

Nutrition Information

- Calories: 363 calories
- Sugar: 28 grams sugar
- Total Fat: 18 grams fat

- Total Carbohydrate: 44 grams carbohydrates
- Saturated Fat: 10 grams saturated fat
- Fiber: 4 grams fiber
- Protein: 2 grams protein
- Sodium: 0.4 milligram of sodium

35. Coconut & Chocolate Macaroons

Serving: Makes 12 | Prep: | Cook: | Ready in:

Ingredients

- 1 egg white
- 200g caster sugar
- 4 tbsp plain flour
- 200g coarsely grated fresh coconut (about 1 coconut in total)
- 150g bar dark chocolate, chopped

Direction

- Heat the oven to 180C/fan 160C/gas 4. In a clean bowl, whisk the egg whites until stiff then gradually add the sugar, whisking continuously until thick and glossy. Sift in the flour, then fold into the egg whites with the coconut until completely combined.
- Using an 8cm pastry cutter, squash spoonfuls of the mixture onto a baking tray lined with non-stick baking paper or silicone plastic sheets - you may need to do this in two batches. Bake for 15-18 mins until golden around the edges and just starting to brown on top. Leave to cool, then transfer to a rack.
- While the macaroons are cooling, melt the chocolate in a microwave or over a pan of hot water and leave to cool slightly. Cover the smooth side with chocolate and leave to set in the fridge. The macaroons will keep in an airtight container for 2 days.

Nutrition Information

- Calories: 206 calories
- Total Carbohydrate: 30 grams carbohydrates
- Sodium: 0.03 milligram of sodium
- Total Fat: 10 grams fat
- Protein: 2 grams protein
- Fiber: 2 grams fiber
- Sugar: 26 grams sugar
- Saturated Fat: 7 grams saturated fat

36. Custard & White Chocolate Biscuits

Serving: Makes about 25 | Prep: 15mins | Cook: 15mins | Ready in:

Ingredients

- 140g butter, softened
- 175g caster sugar
- 1 egg
- ½ tsp vanilla extract
- 225g self-raising flour
- 85g custard powder
- 85g white chocolate, chopped into small chunks

Direction

- Heat oven to 180C/160C fan/gas 4. Line 2-3 baking sheets with baking parchment. Put the butter and sugar in a food processor and whizz until light and fluffy. Add the egg and vanilla, and mix well. Sift together the flour and custard powder, then tip into the bowl and pulse to mix into a dough. Scrape out the food processor and work the chocolate in by hand.
- Roll the dough into balls a little smaller than a walnut, then place on the baking sheets, a little apart to allow for spreading. Press each biscuit down lightly with your fingers.
- Bake for 12-15 mins until lightly golden. Remove and cool on a wire rack.

Nutrition Information

- Calories: 132 calories
- Saturated Fat: 4 grams saturated fat
- Total Carbohydrate: 18 grams carbohydrates
- Sugar: 9 grams sugar
- Protein: 1 grams protein
- Sodium: 0.2 milligram of sodium
- Total Fat: 6 grams fat

37. Easy Chocolate Biscuits

Serving: Makes 25 biscuits | Prep: 25mins | Cook: 15mins | Ready in:

Ingredients

- 250g butter, softened
- 350g light soft brown sugar
- 2 large eggs
- 350g self-raising flour
- 100g cocoa powder
- 200g chocolate chips or chopped chocolate chunks, or 400g for optional dipping (choose your favourite type)

Direction

- Beat the butter and sugar together with an optional pinch of sea salt in a bowl until light and fluffy, then beat in the eggs one at a time. Sift over the flour and cocoa powder and beat into the butter mix, then fold through the chocolate chips. The mix can be made up to 2 days ahead and chilled or frozen for a month, or used straight away.
- To bake, heat oven to 190C/170C fan/gas 5. If the mix is at room temperature, place evenly spaced spoonfuls on parchment-lined baking sheets, allowing 2 tbsp for each cookie. If the mix is fridge cold, you can roll it into 40g balls before baking. The balls can be frozen and the biscuits baked from frozen, but they'll need a few minutes more. Bake for 12-15 mins until spread out and crusty around the outside. Leave to cool slightly and enjoy warm, or leave to cool completely and eat cold. The biscuits will keep in a tin for three days.
- As an optional extra, the biscuits can be dipped in chocolate. To do this, melt your chosen type of chocolate in a bowl over a pan of simmering water or in the microwave. Leave to cool a little, then dip half of each biscuit in the chocolate and leave them on parchment-lined trays somewhere cool to set. Again, the dipped biscuits will keep for up to three days in a tin or lidded plastic container.

Nutrition Information

- Calories: 243 calories
- Sodium: 0.35 milligram of sodium
- Total Carbohydrate: 29 grams carbohydrates
- Total Fat: 12 grams fat
- Protein: 4 grams protein
- Fiber: 1 grams fiber
- Saturated Fat: 7 grams saturated fat
- Sugar: 18 grams sugar

38. Festive Jammie Dodgers

Serving: Makes 24 | Prep: 20mins | Cook: 30mins | Ready in:

Ingredients

- 225g unsalted butter, softened
- 100g caster sugar
- 200g plain flour, plus extra for dusting
- 100g ground almond
- 100g strawberry or raspberry jam (about half a jar)

Direction

- Put the butter, sugar, flour and almonds into a food processor and whizz until the mixture just comes together and forms a ball. If making by hand, first beat together the butter and sugar, then add the flour and ground almonds. Wrap in cling film and leave in the fridge for at least 1 hr.

- Remove the dough from the fridge and knead until it is soft enough to shape and roll. Divide into two even-size balls. Sprinkle a little plain flour over your work surface and roll out one ball of pastry. I find it best to start the rolling myself so that it's even, then let the kids finish it off. The dough should be approximately 5mm thick. Using a star cutter (about 6cm wide) dipped in a little flour to stop it from sticking, cut out as many star shapes as you can. Then lightly knead the dough trimmings together and roll out again. Keep going until you have about 24 stars. Carefully place the stars on a baking sheet, making sure you keep them slightly apart.
- Roll out the second ball of dough the same way. Cut out the same-size stars and place them on a baking sheet. Now cut out a small circle in the centre of each biscuit using a small cookie cutter or the end of a large piping nozzle.
- Heat oven to 140C/fan 120C/gas 1 and cook the biscuits for 20-30 mins until just golden. Remove from the oven and place on a cooling rack to cool completely. Place a blob of jam onto the centre of the biscuits without the cut-out circle. Be generous - you want the jam to show at the edges as well as the centre. Place the top halves of the biscuits on and push down gently. These will keep in an airtight container for up to 3 days.

Nutrition Information

- Calories: 141 calories
- Sodium: 0.01 milligram of sodium
- Fiber: 1 grams fiber
- Protein: 2 grams protein
- Total Fat: 10 grams fat
- Total Carbohydrate: 14 grams carbohydrates
- Sugar: 8 grams sugar
- Saturated Fat: 5 grams saturated fat

39. Freezer Biscuits

Serving: Makes 30 biscuits | Prep: | Cook: 15mins | Ready in:

Ingredients

- 200g pack butter, softened
- 200g soft brown sugar
- 2 eggs
- 1 tsp vanilla extract
- 200g self-raising flour
- 140g oats
- Your choice of flavours
- 50g chopped nuts such as pecan, hazelnuts or almonds
- 50g desiccated coconut
- 50g raisin, or mixed fruit

Direction

- When the butter is really soft, tip it into a bowl along with the sugar. Using an electric hand whisk or exercising some arm muscle, beat together until the sugar is mixed through. Beat in the eggs, one at a time, followed by the vanilla extract and a pinch of salt, if you like. Stir in the flour and oats. The mixture will be quite stiff at this point. Now decide what else you would like to add - any or all of the flavours are delicious - and stir through.
- Tear off an A4-size sheet of greaseproof paper. Pile up half the mixture in the middle of the sheet, then use a spoon to thickly spread the mixture along the centre of the paper. Pull over one edge of paper and roll up until you get a tight cylinder. If you have problems getting it smooth, then roll as you would a rolling pin along a kitchen surface. You'll need it to be about the width of a teacup. When it is tightly wrapped, twist up the ends and then place in the freezer. Can be frozen for up to 3 months.
- To cook, heat oven to 180C/fan 160C/gas 4 and unwrap the frozen biscuit mix. Using a sharp knife, cut off a disk about ½cm wide. If

you have difficulty slicing through, dip the knife into a cup of hot water. Cut off as many biscuits as you need, then pop the mix back into the freezer for another time. Place on a baking sheet, spacing them widely apart as the mixture will spread when cooking, then cook for 15 mins until the tops are golden brown. Leave to cool for at least 5 mins before eating.

Nutrition Information

- Calories: 138 calories
- Total Fat: 8 grams fat
- Protein: 2 grams protein
- Sodium: 0.21 milligram of sodium
- Total Carbohydrate: 16 grams carbohydrates
- Saturated Fat: 5 grams saturated fat
- Sugar: 8 grams sugar
- Fiber: 1 grams fiber

40. Ginger Cookie Sandwiches With Lemon Mascarpone

Serving: Makes 12-15 | Prep: 30mins | Cook: 14mins | Ready in:

Ingredients

- 100g unsalted butter, melted
- 50g golden caster sugar
- 100g light brown soft sugar
- 25g black treacle
- 1 large egg
- ½ tsp vanilla extract
- ¼ tsp bicarbonate of soda
- 175g gluten-free flour blend (I used Doves Farm)
- 1 tbsp ground ginger
- ½ tsp ground black pepper
- ¼ tsp ground nutmeg
- ¼ tsp ground cloves
- ¼ tsp ground cardamom (the seeds from 3 pods, crushed – see tip)
- 75g demerara sugar, to coat
- For the filling
- 175g mascarpone
- 85g lemon curd

Direction

- To make the cookies, put the butter, sugars, treacle, egg and vanilla in a large bowl and mix together with an electric whisk until smooth and combined. In a separate bowl, mix together the remaining ingredients except the demerara. Add the dry ingredients to the egg mixture and mix until a very sticky dough is formed. Cover with cling film and chill for at least 4 hrs.
- Heat oven to 180C/160C fan/gas 4 and line two baking trays with baking parchment. Roll the cookie dough into balls, about a tablespoon in size, then roll in the demerara sugar. Place on the lined trays, leaving about 2.5cm space between cookies.
- Bake for about 14 mins or until just lightly browned around the edges, swapping the trays over halfway through cooking. Allow to cool on the trays for 10 mins before transferring to a wire rack to cool completely.
- To make the filling, beat together the mascarpone and lemon curd in a bowl until smooth and creamy. Transfer to a piping bag fitted with a plain round piping tip. Pipe a layer of the cream onto the base of half the cookies and sandwich together with the other half. Will keep for 3-4 days in a sealed container in the fridge – the texture will turn soft and cakey (this is no bad thing).

Nutrition Information

- Calories: 227 calories
- Saturated Fat: 7 grams saturated fat
- Total Carbohydrate: 28 grams carbohydrates
- Sugar: 18 grams sugar
- Protein: 2 grams protein
- Sodium: 0.1 milligram of sodium
- Total Fat: 12 grams fat

41. Gooey Chocolate Cherry Cookies

Serving: Makes 20 large cookies | Prep: 15mins | Cook: 14mins | Ready in:

Ingredients

- 200g unsalted butter, at room temperature
- 85g light muscovado sugar
- 85g golden caster sugar
- 1 egg
- 225g self-raising flour
- 50g plain chocolate, 50-70% cocoa, roughly chopped
- 50g white chocolate, roughly chopped
- 85g natural colour glacé cherry, roughly chopped

Direction

- Heat oven to 190C/fan 170C/gas 5. Beat the butter, sugars and egg until smooth, then mix in the flour, chocolates and cherry pieces and ½ tsp salt. Spoon onto non-stick baking sheets in large rough blobs - you'll get 20 out of this mix. Make sure they are well spaced as the cookies grow substantially as they bake. The raw dough can be frozen.
- Bake for 12-14 mins until just golden, but still quite pale and soft in the middle. If baking from frozen, give them a few mins more. Cool on the sheets for 5 mins, then lift onto racks with a fish slice and leave to cool completely.

Nutrition Information

- Calories: 186 calories
- Fiber: 1 grams fiber
- Total Fat: 11 grams fat
- Sugar: 14 grams sugar
- Saturated Fat: 6 grams saturated fat
- Protein: 2 grams protein
- Sodium: 0.13 milligram of sodium
- Total Carbohydrate: 23 grams carbohydrates

42. Lemon Sherbet Jammy Dodgers

Serving: Makes 15 | Prep: 45mins | Cook: 15mins | Ready in:

Ingredients

- For the biscuit
- 175g cold slightly salted butter, cubed
- 250g plain flour, plus extra for dusting
- 100g icing sugar
- zest 1 lemon, plus 1-2 tsp juice
- 1 large egg yolk
- 23g pack sherbet (I used Dip Dab)
- For the filling
- 75g slightly salted butter, at room temperature
- 250g icing sugar
- 100g lemon curd

Direction

- In a food processor, whizz the butter, flour and a pinch of salt until the mixture resembles fine breadcrumbs. Add the sugar and lemon zest and whizz again. Add the lemon juice and egg yolk and blend until clumps of dough form around the blades. Keep blending, using the pulse button, until larger balls of dough have formed. Tip out the mixture onto a work surface and knead briefly to bring it together in a smooth ball - don't overwork it or it will be tough. Cut the dough into 2 equal pieces and pat into flat discs, then wrap in cling film and chill for at least 30 mins. Line 2 baking sheets with baking parchment.
- Remove the dough from the fridge 15 mins before you're ready to roll it. Lightly flour your work surface and rolling pin. Unwrap 1 piece of dough and roll it out to the thickness of a 50p piece. Use a 6cm cutter to stamp out discs (you should get about 15) and transfer to a baking sheet using a palette knife.
- Unwrap and roll out the remaining dough to the same thickness. Stamp out 15 discs and

transfer to the second baking sheet. Use a small round cutter (about 1cm) or the end of a piping nozzle to stamp holes from the middle of 15 of the biscuits. Loosely cover the trays with cling film and chill for 15 mins. Heat oven to 180C/160C fan/gas 4.

- Bake the biscuits for 15 mins, swapping the trays over halfway through. Remove from the oven, leave to cool for 5 mins, then transfer to a wire rack and leave to cool completely.
- Meanwhile, make the filling. Place the butter, sugar and half the lemon curd in a bowl. Mash together, then blend with an electric hand whisk. Transfer to a piping bag and snip off the end, making a 1cm opening. Place the remaining lemon curd in another piping bag and snip off the end to make a slightly smaller hole. Dust a little sherbet over the biscuits with a hole in the centre.
- Pipe blobs of lemon filling in a ring shape onto each whole biscuit, leaving space in the centre to fill with lemon curd. Fill the middles, then sandwich a sherbet-dusted biscuit on top of each one. Store in a biscuit tin for 3 days.

Nutrition Information

- Calories: 151 calories
- Total Fat: 7 grams fat
- Saturated Fat: 4 grams saturated fat
- Total Carbohydrate: 20 grams carbohydrates
- Sugar: 13 grams sugar
- Protein: 1 grams protein
- Sodium: 0.1 milligram of sodium

43. Oat Biscuits

Serving: 10 large biscuits or 15 medium ones | Prep: 15mins | Cook: 10mins | Ready in:

Ingredients

- 75g wholemeal flour
- 1 tsp baking powder
- 75g porridge oats
- 50g caster sugar
- 75g butter
- 1 tbsp golden syrup
- 2 tbsp milk

Direction

- Heat the oven to 180C/160C fan/gas 4. Line a baking tray with baking parchment.
- Sift the flour into a bowl. Mix in the baking powder, porridge oats and sugar.
- Melt the butter, syrup and milk in a small saucepan or in the microwave and stir.
- Add to the dry ingredients. Mix until the liquid covers all the oat mixture and until well combined.
- Spoon onto a baking tray and shape into rounds, leaving space between each biscuit as they will spread whilst cooking.
- Bake for 10-15 mins, or until golden brown. Leave to cool for 5 mins before removing from tray.

Nutrition Information

- Calories: 140 calories
- Fiber: 1 grams fiber
- Protein: 2 grams protein
- Sugar: 7 grams sugar
- Sodium: 0.3 milligram of sodium
- Total Fat: 7 grams fat
- Saturated Fat: 4 grams saturated fat
- Total Carbohydrate: 17 grams carbohydrates

44. Oaty Hazelnut Cookies

Serving: makes 9 | Prep: 15mins | Cook: 30mins | Ready in:

Ingredients

- 50g butter, plus a little for greasing
- 2 tbsp maple syrup

- 1 dessert apple, unpeeled and coarsely grated (you need 85g)
- 1 tsp cinnamon
- 50g raisins
- 50g porridge oats
- 50g spelt flour
- 40g unblanched hazelnuts, cut into chunky slices
- 1 egg

Direction

- Heat oven to 180C/160C fan/gas 4 and lightly grease a non-stick baking tray (or line a normal baking tray with baking parchment). Tip the butter and syrup into a small non-stick pan and melt together, then add the apple and cook, stirring, over a medium heat until it softens, about 6-7 mins. Stir in the cinnamon and raisins.
- Mix the oats, spelt flour, and hazelnuts in a bowl, pour in the apple mixture, then add the egg and beat everything together really well.
- Spoon onto the baking tray, well spaced apart to make 9 mounds, then gently press into discs. Bake for 18-20 mins until golden, then cool on a wire rack. Will keep for 3 days in an airtight container or 6 weeks in the freezer.

Nutrition Information

- Calories: 146 calories
- Saturated Fat: 3 grams saturated fat
- Sugar: 8 grams sugar
- Fiber: 2 grams fiber
- Protein: 2 grams protein
- Total Carbohydrate: 15 grams carbohydrates
- Sodium: 0.1 milligram of sodium
- Total Fat: 8 grams fat

45. Pistachio & Cranberry Cookies

Serving: Makes 22 | Prep: 15mins | Cook: 15mins | Ready in:

Ingredients

- 175g butter, softened
- 85g golden caster sugar
- ½ tsp vanilla extract
- 225g plain flour
- 75g pistachios
- 75g dried cranberries

Direction

- Mix the butter, sugar and vanilla extract with a wooden spoon. stir in the flour, then tip in the pistachios and cranberries – you might need to get your hands in at this stage to bring the mix together as a dough. Halve the dough and shape each half into a log about 5cm across. Wrap in cling film, then chill for 1 hr or freeze for up to 3 months.
- Heat oven to 180C/160C fan/gas 4. slice the logs into 1cm-thick rounds, place on a baking tray lined with baking parchment and bake for 12-15 mins. Cool completely on the tray.

Nutrition Information

- Calories: 140 calories
- Protein: 2 grams protein
- Sodium: 0.1 milligram of sodium
- Total Fat: 9 grams fat
- Saturated Fat: 4 grams saturated fat
- Total Carbohydrate: 15 grams carbohydrates
- Sugar: 7 grams sugar

46. Shortbread Recipe

Serving: Makes 24 slices | Prep: 15mins | Cook: 25mins | Ready in:

Ingredients

- 300g butter, softened
- 140g golden caster sugar, plus 4 tbsp
- 300g plain flour
- 140g rice flour

Direction

- Place the butter and 140g sugar in a food processor and whizz until smooth.
- Tip in both the flours and a pinch of salt, then whizz until mixture comes together.
- Using your hands, roughly spread the mixture out in a 20 x 30 x 4cm baking tray. Cover with cling film and smooth over until there are no wrinkles. Place in the fridge, uncooked, for at least 30 mins and up to 2 days.
- Heat oven to 180C/160C fan/gas 4. Remove cling film, then lightly mark the shortbread all over with a fork.
- Sprinkle with the remaining sugar, then bake for 20-25 mins.
- Leave to cool in the tin, then cut into 24 thin slices. Shortbread will keep in an airtight container for up to 1 week.

Nutrition Information

- Calories: 188 calories
- Sodium: 0.2 milligram of sodium
- Total Fat: 11 grams fat
- Saturated Fat: 7 grams saturated fat
- Total Carbohydrate: 23 grams carbohydrates
- Sugar: 9 grams sugar
- Protein: 2 grams protein

47. Sugar Dusted Vanilla Shortbread

Serving: Makes 35 biscuits | Prep: | Cook: 20mins | Ready in:

Ingredients

- 325g plain flour
- 200g chilled salted butter, plus a little more for the sheets
- 125g golden caster sugar
- 2 tsp good-quality vanilla extract
- 2large free range egg yolks
- icing sugar, for dusting

Direction

- Tip the flour into a food processor. Cut the butter into small pieces and drop them into the bowl, then whizz until the mixture looks like breadcrumbs. Add the sugar, vanilla and egg yolks and whizz to a smooth dough.
- With your hands, roll the dough on a lightly floured surface into a sausage shape about 25cm/9in long and 5cm/2½in in diameter. Wrap the roll and chill for at least 1 hour. (The roll can be frozen for up to 6 weeks. To use, remove from the freezer and allow to thaw for one hour at room temperature so that the dough is soft enough to be sliced into biscuits.)
- Preheat the oven to 180C/gas 4/fan 160C and lightly grease 2 large baking sheets. Using a sharp knife, cut the dough into slices, each a generous 5mm/¼in thick, then arrange them on the greased baking sheets, spacing the biscuits slightly apart so they have a bit of room to spread as they cook.
- Bake for 20 minutes until the biscuits are just turning pale golden around the edges, then transfer to a wire rack to cool. Dust generously with icing sugar. The biscuits will keep fresh for up to one week stored in an airtight tin.

48. Sugared Flower Shortbreads

Serving: Makes 15-20 | Prep: 1hours | Cook: 12mins | Ready in:

Ingredients

- 250g plain flour, plus extra for dusting
- 140g cold, slightly salted butter, cut into small cubes
- 85g white caster sugar
- 1 tsp vanilla extract
- 2 egg yolks
- ½ tsp rosewater(optional)

- assortment of 15-20 edible flowers, unsprayed, (we used pansies, violas, primroses and rose petals - see tip)
- 50g caster sugar
- 1 eggwhite, beaten
- 300g royal icing sugarfood colouring pastes (we used yellow, purple and pink)
- edibleshimmer dust (optional)
- tweezers
- 1 small paintbrush
- 8cm biscuit cutter
- 1 disposable piping bag
- 1 fine writing piping nozzle
- tissue paperand a pretty box, to wrap the biscuits in

Direction

- Remove the stalks and any leaves from small flowers like violas or pansies, and carefully pull apart the roses to separate the petals. Place a sheet of baking parchment on your work surface. Sprinkle the caster sugar over a saucer, then lightly whisk the egg white in a small bowl. Holding a flower or petal with tweezers, use a small paintbrush to paint both sides with egg white. Spoon the sugar over, then shake off the excess and place on the parchment. Repeat with the remaining petals or flowers. Leave to dry for 3 hrs, or overnight if you can. Will keep in an airtight container for up to 1 month, but their colour may start to fade after a few weeks.
- Tip the flour into a large bowl and add the butter. Use your fingertips to rub the butter into the flour until you have a damp, crumby texture. Pour in the sugar and gently mix in with your fingertips. Whisk the vanilla, rosewater and egg yolks together in a small bowl with a fork, then drizzle the mixture over the buttery flour. Mix again, squashing the crumbs together to form a dough. If the mixture is a little crumbly, drizzle over 1-2 tsp cold water, then mix again. Tip onto your work surface and knead very briefly until the dough looks even, with no streaks of egg. Wrap in cling film, pat into a round disc and chill for 30 mins.
- Heat oven to 180C/160C fan/gas 4 and line two large baking trays with baking parchment. Remove the dough from the fridge – if it's very firm, leave it at room temperature for 15 mins to soften. Lightly dust the work surface with flour, unwrap the dough and roll it to the thickness of a £1 coin. Stamp out 8cm disks with the fluted side of a biscuit cutter and transfer them to the baking trays. Bake for 10-12 mins, swapping the trays over halfway through cooking. Once lightly golden and firm, remove the biscuits from the oven. Leave to cool on the trays for 10 mins or until stable enough to transfer to a wire rack to cool completely.
- Mix the icing sugar with enough water to make a thick icing. Divide the icing between as many bowls as the number of colours you'd like to use, and dye each one a pastel shade with a drop of food colouring. Transfer half of one of the icings to a disposable piping bag fitted with a fine writing nozzle. Pipe a ring around the outside of the biscuit and set aside to dry. Continue until you've iced a third of the biscuits (if you're using three colours), then move on to the next colour, transferring any leftover icing back to its original bowl. Leave the biscuits to dry for 10-15 mins.
- Add 2-3 tsp water to each icing to make it a little runnier. Spoon the icing onto the biscuits, matching the colour to the rings. Encourage the icing to flood the surface by easing it to the edges with your spoon – don't be too generous with the icing as it may overspill when you add the flowers and petals. You can now dust the surface of each biscuit with a little shimmer dust, if you like, then top with the flowers. Leave the biscuits to set for at least 1 hr before wrapping in tissue paper in a pretty box. Will keep for up to 1 week.

Nutrition Information

- Calories: 193 calories

- Total Carbohydrate: 31 grams carbohydrates
- Protein: 2 grams protein
- Sodium: 0.1 milligram of sodium
- Total Fat: 6 grams fat
- Saturated Fat: 4 grams saturated fat
- Sugar: 22 grams sugar
- Fiber: 1 grams fiber

49. Vegan Shortbread

Serving: Makes 12-14 | Prep: 20mins | Cook: 20mins | Ready in:

Ingredients

- 250g plain flour, plus extra for dusting
- 75g caster sugar, plus 1 tbsp
- ½ tbsp cornflour
- 1 tsp vanilla extract
- 160ml light olive oil

Direction

- Whizz the flour, sugar, a pinch of salt and the cornflour in a food processor to sieve and mix briefly, then add the vanilla and drizzle in the olive oil, pulsing the food processor blades until you get a soft, golden dough. Wrap and chill for 30 mins to rest.
- Heat the oven to 180C/160C fan/gas 4, and line a baking sheet with parchment or a baking mat. Roll the dough out on a lightly floured work surface to a 5mm thickness and use a round or fluted cutter, about 6cm diameter, to cut out shortbread rounds. Use a small palette knife to transfer to the baking sheet. Can be frozen on the baking tray, then transfered to a box when solid. Will keep for up to three months.
- Sprinkle the 1 tbsp sugar over the biscuits and bake for 15-20 mins until golden brown. Leave to cool for a few mins to firm up on the tray, then transfer to a cooling rack to cool completely. Add 2-4 mins to the cooking time if baking from frozen.

Nutrition Information

- Calories: 176 calories
- Saturated Fat: 1 grams saturated fat
- Total Carbohydrate: 21 grams carbohydrates
- Fiber: 1 grams fiber
- Protein: 2 grams protein
- Sodium: 0.03 milligram of sodium
- Total Fat: 9 grams fat
- Sugar: 7 grams sugar

50. Viennese Whirls

Serving: makes 10 | Prep: 45mins | Cook: 12mins | Ready in:

Ingredients

- For the biscuits
- 200g slightly salted butter, softened
- 50g icing sugar
- 2 tsp vanilla extract
- 200g plain flour
- 2 tsp cornflour
- ½ tsp baking powder
- For the filling
- 100g butter, softened
- 170g icing sugar
- 1 tsp vanilla extract
- 50g raspberry jam or strawberry jam

Direction

- Heat oven to 180C/160C fan/gas 4 and line 2 baking sheets with baking parchment. Put the butter and icing sugar in a large bowl and beat with an electric hand whisk for about 5 mins until pale and fluffy. Add the vanilla extract and beat again until fully incorporated.
- Sift in the flour, cornflour and baking powder, and fold into the mixture using a spatula until combined (the dough should have a tacky consistency). Spoon the dough into a piping

bag fitted with a large star-shaped nozzle. If all the mixture doesn't fit, do it in 2 batches.

- Pipe swirly circles 5cm diameter onto 2 baking sheets making sure there are 3cm spaces between each swirl.
- Bake for 10-12 mins, swapping the trays over halfway through the cooking time so the biscuits are evenly baked, until pale golden and cooked through. Leave to cool on the baking sheets for a few mins, then transfer to wire racks.
- While the biscuits cool, make the filling. Put the softened butter in a large mixing bowl and add the icing sugar. Stir together initially with a wooden spoon then switch to electric beaters or a whisk to get the buttercream fluffy and smooth. Add the vanilla extract and beat once more to combine. Transfer the buttercream to a piping bag and snip off the end.
- Turn the biscuits over so their flat side is facing up then pipe buttercream over half of the biscuits and spread a little jam on the rest. Sandwich a jam covered biscuit together with a buttercream one and repeat until all the biscuits are used up.

Nutrition Information

- Calories: 405 calories
- Total Carbohydrate: 42 grams carbohydrates
- Protein: 2 grams protein
- Sugar: 25 grams sugar
- Sodium: 0.6 milligram of sodium
- Saturated Fat: 16 grams saturated fat
- Fiber: 1 grams fiber
- Total Fat: 25 grams fat

Index

A

Almond 3,19

B

Biscuits 3,4,7,10,12,14,16,17,18,23,25,26,27,30

Butter 3,24

C

Cherry 3,6,29

Chocolate 3,5,7,10,11,14,20,22,23,24,25,26,29

Coconut 3,8,25

Cognac 4

Crackers 3,17

Cranberry 3,31

Cream 6,14,17

Curd 3,19

Custard 3,9,25

D

Dab 29

F

Fat 4,5,6,7,8,9,10,11,12,13,14,15,16,17,18,19,20,21,22,23,24,25,26,27,28,29,30,31,32,34,35

Flour 16

Fudge 3,23

G

Gin 3,13,16,19,28

H

Hazelnut 3,11,22,30

Heart 3,6

J

Jam 3,26,29

L

Lemon 3,15,19,28,29

M

Macaroon 3,25

Mascarpone 3,28

Milk 5

N

Nut 4,5,6,7,8,9,10,11,12,13,14,15,16,17,18,19,20,21,22,23,24,25,26,27,28,29,30,31,32,33,34,35

O

Orange 3,9,16

P

Pecan 3,23

Pistachio 3,31

Pulse 16

Pumpkin 3,17

S

Salt 3,17

Shortbread 3,6,9,10,11,24,31,32,34

Sugar 3,4,5,6,7,8,9,10,11,12,13,14,15,16,17,19,20,21,22,23,24,25,26,27,28,29,30,31,32,34,35

T

Tahini 3,20

Tea 27

V

Vegan 3,19,34

Conclusion

Thank you again for downloading this book!

I hope you enjoyed reading about my book!

If you enjoyed this book, please take the time to share your thoughts and post a review on Amazon. It'd be greatly appreciated!

Write me an honest review about the book – I truly value your opinion and thoughts and I will incorporate them into my next book, which is already underway.

Thank you!

If you have any questions, **feel free to contact at:** *author@thymerecipes.com*

Carol Moran

thymerecipes.com

Printed in Great Britain
by Amazon